Contents

		Page
1	Boxing – the Good and the Bad	1
2	Starting Off	4
3	Training	8
4	The Professional	11
5	What Makes a Winner?	15
6	The Will to Win	17
7	Fear	20
8	A Woman's Place?	22
9	The End of the Line	25
	Glossary of Terms	28

When reading this book,
you may come across a word or phrase
that you do not understand.
Check the Glossary on page 28
at the back of this book.
It probably explains it there.

Boxing

Sandra Woodcock

Published in association with The Basic Skills Agency

Hodder & Stoughton

A MEMBER OF THE HODDER HEADLINE GROUP

Acknowledgements

Cover: Steve Bardons/Action-Plus.

Photos: pp. 2, 9, 18 © Allsport; pp. 4, 13 © Action-Plus;
pp. 23, 26 Press Association News Library.

Orders: please contact Bookpoint Ltd, 130 Milton Park, Abingdon, Oxon OX14 4SB. Telephone: (44) 01235 827720. Fax: (44) 01235 400454. Lines are open from 9.00–6.00, Monday to Saturday, with a 24-hour message answering service. Email address: orders@bookpoint.co.uk

British Library Cataloguing in Publication Data
A catalogue record for this title is available from The British Library

ISBN 0 340 74720 X

First published 1999
Impression number 10 9 8 7 6 5 4 3 2
Year   2004 2003 2002 2001

Typeset by Fakenham Photosetting Ltd, Fakenham, Norfolk.
Printed in Great Britain for Hodder & Stoughton Educational, a division of Hodder Headline Plc, 338 Euston Road, London NW1 3BH by The Bath Press, Bath

1 Boxing – the Good and the Bad

Lennox Lewis is a boxer.
One night in Las Vegas in 1993
he won a fight to keep his heavyweight title.
As winner, he took nine million dollars.
Not bad for one night.
Michael Watson is also a boxer.
One night in September 1991
he was fighting Chris Eubank.
One punch from Eubank
sent Watson to death's door.
He was rushed to hospital.
Doctors operated
to remove a blood clot from his brain.
He lay in hospital in a coma for months.
The doctors saved Michael Watson's life
but only just.

That's boxing.
The game can give the boxer
fame, glory and big money.
But the risk is very serious injury or
even death.

Lennox Lewis and Tony 'TNT' Tucker,
Las Vegas 1993.

What does it take to get to the top,
to be a millionaire by the time you are 21?
What does it take
to walk away with all the prizes
and keep your face and body unmarked?

One thing is for sure.
It takes more than hard punching.
It takes skill and hard work,
quick thinking and self-control.
A good boxer can survive in the ring.
You also need to be good at
the business side of the game.
It's a tough world in and out of the ring.

2 Starting Off

Most boxers start off by going to a gym.
Some turn up by chance
and end up trying out in the ring.
Some hang around at the gym
as young kids and get started that way.
Others might be sent to the gym
because they have some talent at fighting.
But the gym is the starting place.

It's a place to train.
You can spar with other boxers.
You can find out if you can hit
and if you can stand being hit.

The gym is a place to watch other boxers.
You pick up skills and tips
and find out what it's all about.

Kids with talent
are soon spotted by trainers.
The trainer is on the look out
for new boxers with promise.
The trainer can help
to develop skills and confidence.

Training in the gym.

A boxing career starts with amateur fights.
The trainers set up fights for their boxers.
It's a way to gain experience.

Amateur boxing is hard.
The boxer has to put in hours of training.
He has to keep fit and do his best.
But there is no pay.
Amateur boxers may have other jobs
and have to fit training hours
into their day as well.

Amateurs can make a name for themselves
if they are good.
In World Boxing, the best amateurs
may go to the Olympic Games.
Lennox Lewis won an Olympic gold medal
and went professional after that.
He was able to earn good money right away.
He was a champion
from the beginning of his career.

Most boxers who turn professional
never make it to the top.
Many spend all of their careers
in small-time fights or on the undercard.
They may earn a few hundred pounds
every few months.
But they still have to put in
the hard work to keep fit.
They still have to take the beatings,
the cuts, puffed eyes and broken noses.
Boxing can be tough work
with little fame or gain.

3 Training

The first rule of any sport is fitness.
A boxer has to be fit
because he has to protect himself.
In the ring he is on his own
against an opponent who wants to hurt him.
So boxers work hard to keep fit.

This means training every day.
It means running,
often early in the morning.
It means long tough work-outs.

To keep fit and improve skills
a boxer must practise in the ring,
sparring with other boxers.

A boxer also has to keep
a close watch on his weight.
Before every fight there is a weigh-in.
The boxer cannot weigh more
than the maximum weight for his class.

Prince Naseem at the weigh-in.

If he is in the lightweight class,
he cannot weigh more
than 135 pounds (61.2 kg).
But if he is below 126 pounds,
then he will be in the featherweight class.
So a boxer must watch everything
he eats and drinks just before a fight.

Prince Naseem was once
three pounds overweight
just two days before his fight.
He went without food for 36 hours.
He got his weight down
in time for the weigh-in.
This is where self-control comes in.
A boxer has to be strong in mind
as well as in body.

4 The Professional

A boxer can earn money from fighting
if he turns professional.

The fights will be harder
and he will need to pace himself
for more rounds.
If a boxer decides to turn professional,
he has to have a licence to fight.
In Britain the licence comes from
the British Boxing Board of Control.

The boxer has to pass medical tests,
brain scans and eye tests
before he can get a licence.
Now the tests are more difficult.
There are written tests as well.

Once a boxer has his licence to fight
he will sign a contract with a manager.
The manager arranges fights for him
and looks after his interests.

The manager will take
between 25 and 30 per cent
of the boxer's earnings.
The trainer will get about 10 per cent.
So they will try to arrange fights
with big prize money.

The biggest prize money
is in world title fights.
These titles come from
different boxing organizations.
There are world titles sponsored by
the World Boxing Association (WBA),
the World Boxing Council (WBC),
the World Boxing Organization (WBO),
and the International Boxing Federation (IBF).
So a heavyweight fighter
could be world champ with a WBC title.
Another fighter might be
World Heavyweight Champion
with a WBA title.
The only way to be sure
of being number one
is to win all the titles.

Mike Tyson at the WBC heavyweight title fight,
Las Vegas.

Fighters who make it to the top
win big prize money.
They can also get money
from advertising.
Prince Naseem has linked his name
with Joe Bloggs clothes,
with computer games,
with Audi cars and many others.

When you are at the top,
there is plenty of money, fast cars,
lots of offers, lots of friends.
There are plenty of people
who will use a boxer.
They will get what they can out of him,
and then leave him
when the money stops coming in.
Bad contracts can leave a fighter
with no control over his career.
He has to fight when and where he is told.
Lennox Lewis made sure that his contract
gave him the last word on these things.
To stay in control you have to stay on top,
in and out of the ring.

5 What Makes a Winner?

Training develops the skills of boxing:
fast footwork and hand movements,
strong joints and stamina.
To be a winner
you have to build on the training.

In boxing you are on your own in the ring.
You cannot depend on other team mates
if you are not at your best.
They can't send on a sub
if things start to go wrong.
A good boxer knows he has to rely
on his own skills and tactics.

He will study his opponent before a fight.
He will watch fight videos
to see how his opponent punches.
He will try to find
the other boxer's weak points.

Lennox Lewis once had to fight an opponent
who had an eye injury.
It was his weak point.
When Lewis trained,
his sparring partners wore
a cross of white tape
just above the right eye.
Lewis trained to hit that spot every time.
It sounds cruel, but it is what boxers do.
If they sense a weakness, they go for it.

A good boxer has many moves
and combinations of punches.
He tries to surprise his opponent.
It is hard to predict what he will do.

6 The Will to Win

Good boxers train, keep fit
and prepare for their fights.
To be a winner takes more.
One trainer, who has trained
champions like Tyson and Lewis,
said: 'Boxing is a contest of will and skill.
The will generally overcomes the skill,
unless the skill of one man
is much greater than the skill of the other.'

If two boxers are evenly matched,
will power can decide the outcome.
True champions have great self-confidence.
They do not consider losing.
Naseem says he is 'born to be king.'
Muhammed Ali used to say
'I am the greatest.'
Some, like Lennox Lewis,
have a quiet confidence.
He is often so calm before a fight
that he can fall asleep just before it starts.

Muhammed Ali was very confident.

Lewis plays chess.
He thinks of boxing as a bit like
a game of chess.
In a fight he has to choose his tactics
to solve a problem.
In chess, as in boxing,
two opponents face each other,
each one trying to win.

When he was training to fight Razor Ruddock,
Lewis changed his training timetable
and his sleeping pattern.
He needed his body to be ready to fight
in the middle of the night.
This was because the fight was to be
in the middle of the night.
Ruddock stuck to his usual training times.
It was just one thing
that may have helped Lennox Lewis to win.

A champion has to do more
than keep fit and hit hard.
He has to use his brain.

7 Fear

Many people say that boxing is too brutal.
Some would like the sport to be banned.
Others say that boxers
should not be allowed to hit the head
because of the danger of brain injury.
Muhammed Ali has Parkinson's Disease.
It could have been caused
by getting punched.
Other boxers have had brain damage
or bad eye injuries.
Boxing is the only sport
where you could legally kill your opponent.

The referee can stop a fight
if he thinks one of the boxers
is too badly hurt.
A boxer can lose his licence to fight
if he doesn't stick to the rules.
This happened to Mike Tyson
because he bit a chunk
out of his opponent's ear.

Every boxer must fear the worst
when he goes into the ring.
But the best have learned
to cope with that fear.
Lennox Lewis says it is just a job.
'If you are doing the job
you are trained for,
fear doesn't come into it.'

8 A Woman's Place?

Is boxing a man's sport?
Is there a place for women fighters
in the ring?
People have strong views about this.
Some say that women should be able to box
if they want to.
Others say boxing is not for women.

In America and in some other countries,
women's boxing is allowed.
But the British Boxing Board of Control (BBBC)
has refused to allow it.
Britain's only woman professional boxer,
Jane Couch, was refused a licence to fight.
She has fought in the USA
and won a world title in 1996.
But she was not allowed to fight in Britain.

Jane Couch wins her case.

The BBBC said that boxing
was too dangerous for women.
If women were punched in the chest,
they could get breast cancer.
Others said that boxing fans
did not want to see women in the ring.
It was said that women were not able
to control their moods as well as men.
So boxing wasn't right for them.

But Jane Couch and her lawyer
took the BBBC to court.
She won her case
and won the right to a licence.
The BBBC had to pay her £15,000.
Jane was pleased for herself
and for other women who want to box.

9 The End of the Line

Boxing is not a game for old men.
Most boxers will be ready to retire
in their mid-thirties.
Their dream is to make good money
and maybe invest it for the future.
They want to retire rich and in good shape.
But that's hard.
Too often the money runs out.

Bad business deals can mean
that a boxer has a good life
while he's fighting
but is left with nothing if he stops.
The end can come quickly.
You start to lose fights,
you start to slide
and suddenly it's all over.

The very famous
can sometimes live off their names.
Joe Louis ended his days
as a tourist attraction at Caesar's Palace.
Sitting in a wheelchair,
he posed for photos with tourists.

Frank Bruno appeared in pantomime
when he retired.

Many of the heroes of boxing
came from poor families.
They saw a chance to use their fists
to fight their way out of poverty.
Many kids today dream of doing the same.

But boxing is a hard life.
There are thrills, glamour,
big money and fame to be won.
But there is also blood, sweat, pain,
fear and failure.
For every boxer who has a world title
how many bite the dust?

Glossary of Terms

WBA   World Boxing Association

WBC   World Boxing Council

WBO   World Boxing Organization

IBF   International Boxing Federation

BBBC British Boxing Board of Control

on the undercard   When there is a fight
between two famous boxers, there will often
be less important fights first.
These are warm-ups to the big events.
The boxers in these fights
are 'on the undercard'.

sparring   This is fight practice in the ring.
When training, a boxer will have
a 'sparring partner.'